Milton Hershey

Community BUILDERS

Milton Hershey

Chocolate King, Town Builder

by Charnan
Simon

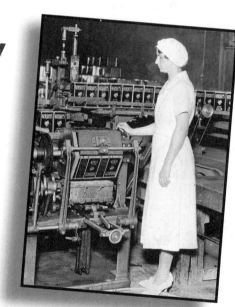

Children's Press®
A Division of Grolier Publishing
New York London Hong Kong Sydney
Danbury, Connecticut

Photo Credits

Photographs ©: Archive Photos: 8, 14, 16, 43; Brown Brothers: 3; Culver Pictures: 23; Daemmrich/The Image Works: 44; Hershey Community Archives: back cover, 10 right, 12, 15, 17, 18, 19, 20 bottom, 24, 25, 27 top, 28, 30, 31, 32, 34, 37, 38, 39, 40; Hershey Foods Corporation: 7, 42; Joe Benson: 27 bottom; Superstock, Inc.: 26, 45; Tom Kazunas: 48; UPI/Corbis-Bettmann: cover, 2, 6, 10 left, 20 top.

Reading Consultant
Linda Cornwell, Learning Resource Consultant
Indiana Department of Education

Visit Children's Press on the Internet at:
http://publishing.grolier.com

Library of Congress Cataloging-in-Publication Data

Simon, Charnan.
    Milton Hershey : chocolate king, town builder / by Charnan Simon.
       p. cm. — (Community builders)
    Includes bibliographical references and index.
    Summary: Relates the story of the founder of the Hershey Chocolate Company in Hershey, Pennsylvania, known for his hard work, perseverance, and charity on behalf of young people.
    ISBN: 0-516-20389-4 (lib. bdg.)   0-516-26330-7 (pbk.)
    1. Hershey, Milton Snavely, 1857-1945—Juvenile literature. 2. Businessmen—United States—Biography—Juvenile literature. 3. Hershey Foods Corporation—History—Juvenile literature. 4. Chocolate industry—United States—History—Juvenile literature. 5. Candy industry—United States—History—Juvenile literature. 6. Hershey (Pa.)—History—Juvenile literature. [1. Hershey, Milton Snavely, 1857-1945. 2. Confectioners. 3. Businessmen. 4. Hershey (Pa.)] I. Title. II. Series.
HD9200.U52H476 1998
338.7'664153'092—dc21
[B]   97-24560
                                                CIP
                                                AC

Contents

Chapter ONE

"If at First You Don't Succeed..."

Milton Hershey

Have you ever had a really wonderful idea, but you couldn't make it work? No matter how hard you tried, it just never turned out the way you wanted it to. There is an old saying, "If at first you don't succeed, try, try again." This can be difficult advice to follow. When you keep failing, you want to give up.

One man who knew all about trying and failing was Milton Snavely Hershey. He tried to set up his own business many times. Each time he failed miserably. He lost all of his own money and the money of his friends and family. But Milton was stubborn. He knew he had a good idea, and he was determined to make it work.

Today, we can all be grateful for Milton Hershey's stubbornness. His good idea was the

Hershey Foods Corporation makes many tasty treats.

Hershey Chocolate Company. Thanks to Milton's hard work and determination, we have Hershey's candy bars, chocolate syrup, cocoa, and other treats to sweeten up our world!

Milton Hershey made a lot of money from his chocolate company. He wanted to use his money in a worthwhile way. Instead of spending it all on himself, he used his money to help other people.

Milton Hershey built an entire town called Hershey, Pennsylvania. In this town he built homes, schools, and churches. He also built theaters, swimming pools, a sports arena, and an amusement park.

Perhaps most importantly, Milton Hershey started a school for disadvantaged children. Milton knew what it was like to be young and penniless. He had no children of his own, but that didn't stop him from wanting to help other children. He gave his entire personal fortune to the school that is named after

Hershey Stadium is just one of many places built in Hershey, Pennsylvania, for the townspeople to enjoy.

Philanthropist

Milton Hershey was a philanthropist. A philanthropist is a person who helps others by giving them money and other things they need. A philanthropist doesn't expect to receive anything in return.

him. Today, the Milton Hershey School serves more than one thousand boys and girls.

Milton Snavely Hershey was born in the little town of Derry, Pennsylvania, on September 13, 1857. Milton's family had lived in the rolling hills of central Pennsylvania for more than one hundred years. His great-grandfather built the farmhouse, called The Homestead, in which Milton was born.

Milton didn't live in the comfortable stone farmhouse for long, however. His father, Henry, was a dreamer. Henry couldn't seem to settle down to any one job or place to live. He moved his family many times during Milton's childhood.

9

Young Milton (left) attended this one-room schoolhouse (above) called the Derry Church School.

All of this moving made it hard for Milton to get an education. By the time he was thirteen years old, he had attended six different schools. But Milton's father loved books and reading. He wanted his son to keep going to school. Milton's mother Fanny, however, was more practical. She thought it was time for her son to learn a trade.

Milton's mother and father came to an agreement. Milton would leave school and become a printer's apprentice. An apprentice is a young person who is learning a trade from a skilled person. In

10

Trade

A trade is a job or craft that requires working with your hands or with machines. Carpenters, electricians, mechanics, and printers are all people who have learned a trade.

Milton Hershey's day, an apprentice usually lived with the person he worked for. Milton's mother was pleased that her son would be learning a trade. His father was happy that Milton would be surrounded by writing and newspapers.

Unfortunately, Milton wasn't a very good printer's apprentice. After two years, Fanny Hershey found another job for her son. Milton would learn to make candy in Joe Royer's Ice Cream Parlor and Garden in Lancaster, Pennsylvania.

Milton liked candy making from the beginning. It was a tricky business, since there were no exact

11

recipes to follow. Joe Royer taught his young apprentice to start with sugar, then add water and flavorings. He showed Milton how to let the mixture boil

Henry and Fanny Hershey, Milton's parents

until just the right moment. Then, together, Joe and Milton poured the candy out onto a big marble counter to cool.

Milton learned that he had a special knack for making candy. Customers liked his caramels and peppermints and fudge. After a few years, Milton decided he had learned all he could from Joe Royer. It was time to start his own candy business.

By the time he was sixteen years old, Milton was an apprentice candy maker.

Chapter TWO

"M. S. Hershey, Dealer in Fine Confectionery"

Nineteen-year-old Milton Hershey decided to start his candy business in Philadelphia, Pennsylvania. Philadelphia was an exciting place to be in 1876. The city was celebrating the 100th anniversary of the signing of the Declaration of Independence. Thousands of people would be visiting the city for the celebration. Milton Hershey wanted to sell his candy to all those people.

One of the many parades held in Philadelphia to celebrate the 100th anniversary of American independence

Philadelphia, Pennsylvania

Philadelphia is known as "The Birthplace of the United States." The Declaration of Independence and the Constitution of the United States were both signed in the city's historic Independence Hall. Today, Philadelphia is home to one and a half million people.

Milton borrowed money from his Uncle Abraham and set up his candy shop. With his mother and his Aunt Mattie to help, he began cooking, wrapping, and delivering his candies. He printed up fancy business cards to help advertise his candies. "M. S. Hershey, Dealer in Fine Confectionery, Fruits, Nuts, [and more]" read the cards—and how proud Milton was of them!

Milton Hershey's first business card

No matter how hard Milton worked, he did not make enough money to pay his bills. He had to borrow more money from his Uncle Abraham, but it still wasn't enough. Milton worked so hard that he made himself sick. Finally, he had to admit his first business was a failure.

Although Milton was discouraged, he didn't give up. He had heard that the West was a good place for a young man to make his fortune. Milton told his mother and Aunt Mattie good-bye and moved to Denver, Colorado.

Fresh milk, which was delivered by horse-drawn cart before cars were invented, became an important ingredient in Milton's chocolates.

Milton's candy business in Denver failed, too. But he did learn an important candy-making secret. He learned that fresh milk makes good candy. This secret didn't help Milton much in Denver. But it would help him a lot a few years later.

After Denver, Milton tried his luck in Chicago, New Orleans, and New York. Everywhere he went,

16

the same thing happened. No matter how hard he worked, he couldn't seem to make enough money to pay his bills.

Tired, broke, and discouraged, Milton Hershey finally moved home to Pennsylvania in 1886. He was twenty-nine years old. He felt as if he would never have a chance to use his business cards.

Workers outside Milton's candy shop in Philadelphia

Chapter THREE

Success at Last

Milton's Aunt Mattie

Milton didn't get a very warm welcome back in Lancaster. His Uncle Abraham refused to loan him any more money. Even Milton's mother and loyal Aunt Mattie couldn't help him. But Milton refused to give up. He scraped together enough money to start up yet another candy business.

Milton Hershey's early candy products

This time luck was with Milton. His caramel candies—made with fresh milk—were a great success. An Englishman was so impressed with the candies, he ordered a huge supply to be shipped to England. Milton knew the milk would keep his candy fresh even after weeks on an ocean liner. The secret he had learned in Denver was starting to pay off.

Before he knew it, Milton had more business than he could handle. He borrowed money from the Lancaster National Bank to buy more candy-making equipment. This time, Milton had no trouble paying back the loan.

Left: As a result of the company's success, Milton was named one of Lancaster's Most Important Citizens in 1889.

Below: Lancaster Caramel Company, about 1889, where Milton achieved his first great success

Business kept booming. Everyone seemed to be eating the caramels Milton was making in his Lancaster Caramel Company. There were so many to choose from! McGinties, Jim Cracks, and Roly Polies for the children. Lotuses, Paradox, and Cocoanut Ices for adults. Melbas, Empires, and Icelets for people who liked their candies made with skimmed milk instead of smooth, rich cream. And all of the different shapes and flavors were invented by Milton Hershey himself.

Soon Milton had to expand. He built factories in other Pennsylvania cities. He started a branch in New York City, and another in Chicago. He shipped his caramels all over the country—and soon, all over the world. People everywhere—Japan, China, Australia, and Europe—loved Milton's caramels.

The Lancaster Caramel Company made Milton Hershey a rich man. But it wasn't caramels that made him famous. In 1893, Milton had an idea that would make "Hershey" a household name around the world.

Chapter FOUR

"I Want to Make Chocolate"

It all started when Milton visited the World's Columbian Exposition in Chicago. Milton was fascinated by an exhibition of chocolate-making equipment from Germany. He studied the machinery for hours. Then he made up his mind. He would buy the equipment, ship it to Lancaster, and start making chocolate himself.

Making chocolate was harder than it looked. Milton and his candy makers tried one recipe after

22

World's Columbian Exposition

The 1893 World's Columbian Exposition in Chicago was held to celebrate the 400th anniversary of Christopher Columbus's arrival in North America. It was a giant world's fair, with exhibits from around the globe. More than 27,000,000 people visited the exposition.

One of the buildings Milton visited at the exposition

Milton decided to build his chocolate factory in the farm country near his hometown.

another, until they found just the taste they wanted. Eventually, Milton's factory was making 114 different kinds of fancy chocolates. Then, in 1900, Milton Hershey made a big decision. He didn't want to run both a caramel factory and a chocolate factory. From then on, he would only make chocolates.

On August 10, 1900, Milton Hershey sold the Lancaster Caramel Company for $1 million. He immediately began plans to build a huge new chocolate factory. This factory would be located out in the farmland near Milton's birthplace in Derry, Pennsylvania.

Building a factory in the middle of the cornfields made sense to Milton Hershey. There was plenty of land to build on. There was plenty of fresh water. And there were plenty of cows to provide good, fresh milk for making delicious chocolates.

Kitty Hershey, around the time she married Milton (1898)

Not everyone agreed with Milton. His wife, Kitty, told him he ought to have his head examined. Everyone knew that factories belonged in cities! Besides, she would ask, where would the factory workers live—in a barn?

But Milton Hershey had thought of that, too. He promptly began to build a town for his workers. There would be comfortable houses with gardens. There would also be schools, churches, and stores. There would be a post office and a trolley car for transportation. It would be a wonderful town—and it would eventually be named Hershey, Pennsylvania.

Trolley Cars

Trolley cars, or streetcars, are a sort of passenger train that roll along rails in city streets. The cars are run by overhead power lines.

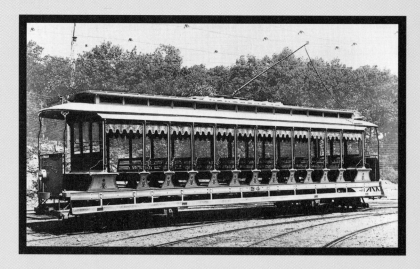

Above: The first houses in Milton's town were built on Trinidad Avenue.

Right: Many of the streets of Milton's town were given names that refer to chocolate.

It all happened just the way Milton Hershey said it would. The Hershey Chocolate Company was soon bigger than anyone could have imagined. And Hershey, Pennsylvania, grew into a thriving town with two main streets—named Chocolate and Cocoa Avenues!

27

The Hershey Chocolate factory, where Milton first concentrated on making only one product—a chocolate bar

Chapter FIVE

The Hershey Chocolate Company

There were several reasons the Hershey Chocolate Company was so successful. For one thing, Milton Hershey decided to specialize. Instead of making 114 different kinds of fancy candies, he would make just one—a simple milk chocolate candy bar. But he decided to make so many of these bars that they would be cheap to buy. Instead of being an expensive luxury for rich people, Hershey's chocolate bars would be a treat everyone could afford.

29

Milton paid $2,000 for his first automobile and used it to advertise his chocolate.

Milton Hershey also knew how to advertise his chocolate. For starters, he bought the very first automobile in Lancaster. (The automobile was still a new invention when the Hershey Chocolate factory was completed in

Chocolate

Chocolate is made from the seeds of the cacao tree. Cacao seeds—or cocoa beans, as we know them—grow in warm, moist climates in Africa, South America, and Malaysia. By themselves, cocoa beans taste bitter. But when they are roasted and mixed with sugar (and with milk, for milk chocolate), they make a delicious, sweet treat!

1905.) Milton painted "Hershey's Cocoa" on the side of the car and drove all around town making deliveries. Then he sent the car on a tour around the state of Pennsylvania. Everywhere it stopped, crowds gathered. They came to see the automobile, but they left with an order of chocolate.

Milton also printed posters and counter displays. Many of these advertisements showed pictures of green pastures and happy cows and healthy, wholesome milk. Who wouldn't want to eat a delicious, nutritious treat like a Hershey's milk chocolate bar?

Eventually, the Hershey Chocolate Company sold a few other chocolate items. There were chocolate bars with nuts in them. There were chocolate bars with

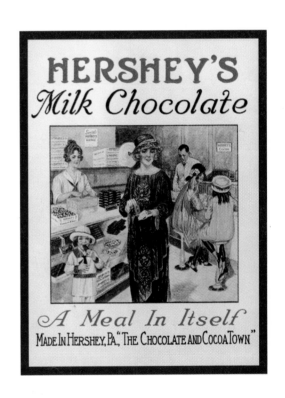

An advertisement for Hershey's Milk Chocolate

Introduced in 1907, Hershey's Kisses™ are still popular. Here, a worker inspects some of the eighty million Kisses™ produced each day.

crisped cereal inside. And in 1907, Milton Hershey invented a tasty little piece of chocolate wrapped in silver foil—the Hershey's Kiss™. Hershey also sold cocoa, chocolate coatings for other candies, baking chocolate, and chocolate syrup.

Milton was a very smart businessman. For example, the most expensive part of making chocolate was buying sugar. Once Milton lost a lot of money on a large sugar deal. He never wanted that to happen again. So he started growing and processing his own sugarcane on the island of Cuba.

32

Hershey, Pennsylvania

Hershey is nestled in the rolling hills of south-eastern Pennsylvania. Today, it is home to almost 12,000 people. Many of them work for the Hershey Foods Corporation or one of its tourist attractions. With a theme park, wildlife center, museum and visitors' center, extensive gardens, and resort hotels, Hershey is an exciting place to visit any time of year.

Inhabitants of Milton's town enjoy one of the parks Milton provided.

Besides knowing a lot about chocolates and the business world, Milton Hershey knew a lot about people. He had a talent for hiring the best people to work for him. He tried hard to keep his employees happy.

The town Milton built for his workers is a good example of the way Milton cared about them. He provided water, electricity, and gas. He built parks, gardens, an amusement park, and a zoo. He also arranged to have a train line and a post office built. He tried to think of everything the perfect town would need.

34

During the Great Depression of the 1930s, Hershey kept his workers busy building a Community Center, a hotel, a Junior-Senior High School, and a huge new sports stadium. He was very proud of the fact that none of his employees lost their jobs during the Depression.

But even Milton Hershey sometimes had problems. Some of his workers thought he was too bossy. He built them nice houses—but some of the workers wanted to build their own houses. He planned a nice town for them to live in—but he didn't ask what they wanted their town to include. Still, most of his workers knew how hard he tried to be a fair boss.

The Great Depression

A depression is a time when businesses fail and many workers lose their jobs. The Great Depression in the United States lasted from 1929 through the 1930s. During this time, one-third of all workers in the United States lost their jobs.

Chapter SIX

"It's Kitty's Idea"

B y 1909, Milton and Kitty Hershey knew they had more money than they could ever spend on themselves. They wanted to use their money to help others. Kitty suggested that they start a school for orphaned boys. Kitty and Milton had always been sad that they had no children of their own. They were both glad for the chance to help other children.

The Hersheys immediately began making plans. They wanted to give their orphans a safe, secure place to live. They also wanted to teach the boys how to earn a living when they grew up. Milton remembered how hard it had been for him to be successful

Milton and Kitty
(left) built a
twenty-room
mansion called
High Point
(below). But they
also wanted to use
their money to
help others,
especially children.

Milton sits on the steps of the Hershey Industrial School with some of the boys he and Kitty helped.

at a job he liked. He hoped his school would make life easier for "his" boys.

The Hershey Industrial School opened in 1909, in the old stone farmhouse where Milton was born. The first two students were brothers, ages four and six. More boys followed. Before long, The Homestead wasn't big enough to hold them all. New buildings were added. Soon these, too, were filled with busy, happy boys.

In 1915, Kitty Hershey died after a long illness. Milton was heartbroken. In 1918, he decided to give his entire personal fortune—about $60 million—to the school that was Kitty's idea.

Today, the name of the school has been changed to the Milton Hershey School. Girls and boys both go there now—more than one thousand of them!

Girls and boys of all ages attend the Milton Hershey School.

Milton Hershey, just a few years before his death in 1945

Milton Hershey died on October 13, 1945. He had seen many changes in his eighty-eight years. He had grown from a penniless young man to one of the richest men in the country. His chocolate factory in Hershey, Pennsylvania, is still the world's largest chocolate manufacturing plant.

The E. Award

In 1942, Milton Hershey received the Army and Navy E. Award for his Field Ration D bar. (A ration is a food allowance for one day.) From 1941 to 1945, the United States was fighting in World War II. The Hershey Chocolate Company made a special candy bar for Americans fighting in the war. This Field Ration D bar was made with extra nutrients and vitamins. It was given to every U.S. soldier and sailor as a sort of emergency meal in a wrapper.

Tour rides give visitors a chance to see how chocolate is made. Free samples are offered at the end of the tour!

Today, you can visit Hershey, Pennsylvania, and learn more about Milton Hershey and his chocolates. You can see the museum, the amusement park, the zoo, and the beautiful gardens. In the visitor's center, you can even take a tour of a pretend chocolate factory.

You can also visit the nearby Milton Hershey School. The fortune that Milton Hershey earned making chocolate is still at work there, giving thousands of children a safe home and a good education. It is a monument that Milton would be proud of.

More than thirty million guests visit Hershey's
Chocolate World each year.

In Your Community

Milton Hershey had to try again and again before he finally figured out the best way to make and sell chocolates. Is there something that you have been trying to do that doesn't seem to be working out? Can you try again? Maybe a grownup can help you think of a new way to look at the problem.

Milton Hershey liked helping people. He left all of his money to his school for poor, orphaned boys. Do you get an allowance? Could you earn money by doing chores around the house? Ask a grownup to help you

Timeline

1857 — Milton S. Hershey is born on September 13 in Derry, Pennsylvania.

1870 — Milton is apprenticed to a newspaper printer.

1872 — Milton is apprenticed to Joe Royer, candy maker.

1876 — Milton moves to Philadelphia to start his own candy business.

1882 — Milton leaves Philadelphia; he tries to succeed as a candy maker in Denver, Chicago, New Orleans, and New York.

1886 — Milton moves back to Lancaster, Pennsylvania; he starts the Lancaster Caramel Company.

1893 — Milton visits the World's Columbian Exposition in Chicago; he purchases chocolate-making equipment.

1894 — Milton begins making chocolates as well as caramels.

1898 — Milton marries Catherine (Kitty) Sweeney.

find ways to help other children with your money. (Today, there are not many homes for orphans in the United States. But there are homeless shelters and food pantries.)

Milton Hershey built a whole town. How can you make your town or city a better place to live? Can you volunteer to clean up a local park? Can you pass out neighborhood newsletters? Can you help your parents in a community service activity? Perhaps you can help deliver Meals-On-Wheels, or take library books to people who cannot leave their homes. Ask a grownup for other ideas.

Milton begins work on a new factory and a town for his workers.

Milton's new town is officially named Hershey, Pennsylvania

Milton and Kitty found Hershey Industrial School for orphaned boys.

Milton pledges his entire fortune to Hershey Industrial School (later renamed Milton Hershey School).

1900 **1903** **1905** **1906** **1907** **1909** **1915** **1918** **1945**

Milton sells the Lancaster Caramel Company; he decides to make and sell only chocolates.

The Hershey Chocolate Company is completed.

Hershey's Kisses™ are introduced.

Kitty Hershey dies.

Milton Hershey dies on October 13 at the age of eighty-eight.

To Find Out More

Here are some additional resources to help you learn more about Milton Hershey, chocolate, and the state of Pennsylvania:

Books

Burford, Betty. *Chocolate By Hershey.* Carolrhoda Books, 1994.

Fradin, Dennis Brindell. *Pennsylvania.* Children's Press, 1994.

Malone, Mary. *Milton Hershey, Chocolate King.* Garrard Publishing Company, 1971.

Morton, Marcia. *Chocolate, An Illustrated History*. Crown Publishers, 1986.

Norman, Jill. *Chocolate.* Bantam, 1990.

O'Neill, Catherine. *Let's Visit a Chocolate Factory.* Troll Associates, 1988.

Video

Chocolate, Chocolate, Chocolate. Best Film and Video Corporation, 1990.

Organizations and Online Sites

Milton Hershey School
P. O. Box 830
Hershey, PA 17033-0830

Hershey Vacation Guide
100 W. Hersheypark Drive
Hershey, PA 17033
http://www.800hersheys.com

Hershey Foods Corporation
Hershey, PA 17033
http://www.hersheys.com/ visitors.html

Hershey Museum
http://www.hershey-museum. microserve.net/
Here you'll find information about exhibits that tell the story of Milton Hershey's life. The museum also has exhibits that detail the cultural heritage of the Germans who settled the area of Pennsylvania where Milton was born. There are many other interesting collections here, too!

Index

About the Author

Charnan Simon lives in Madison, Wisconsin, with her husband, Tom Kazunas, and her daughters, Ariel and Hana. She is a former editor of *Cricket* magazine and has written many books for young readers.

Charnan has been a fan of Milton Hershey for her entire life. She bought—and ate—several large bags of Hershey's Miniatures™ as inspiration in writing this book.